THIS BOOK BELONGS TO:

_____

Favorite Color: _____

Dream Travel Destination: _____

Alter Ego: _____

Never ask me to... _____

I can't live without... _____

If you find this book, please ...

_____

_____

_____

 = **Take a pic for the lockscreen of your dreams.**

This book is for the deep thinkers, the emotional, and people constantly overcoming obstacles who remain authentic.
—JP

An imprint of Bonnier Publishing USA | 251 Park Avenue South, New York, NY 10010 | Copyright © 2018 by Jessie Paege
Text by Aubre Andrus | All art by Kristin Noble except for images on page 58 and 83 | Cover and additional photography by Jon Sams
Photography on page 62 by Jessie Paege (left) and Jerry Maestas (right) | All rights reserved, including the right of reproduction in whole or in part in any form. Sizzle Press is a trademark of Bonnier Publishing USA, and associated colophon is a trademark of Bonnier Publishing USA.
Manufactured in China TPL1217 | First Edition
1 3 5 7 9 10 8 6 4 2
ISBN 978-1-4998-0721-9
sizzlepressbooks.com | bonnierpublishingusa.com

Jessie Paege

Hi everyone,

I'm very lucky to have built my career on creativity. It all started with my own YouTube channel and branched out from there. Even as a kid and every step of the way since then, I've followed my creative vision. I want that for you too.

This book is for getting out the artistic ideas you didn't even know you had. It's for getting in touch with your emotions. It allows you to briefly escape.

Use this book to develop your creative vision, or to fuel your artistic drive.

Enjoy!

Jessie

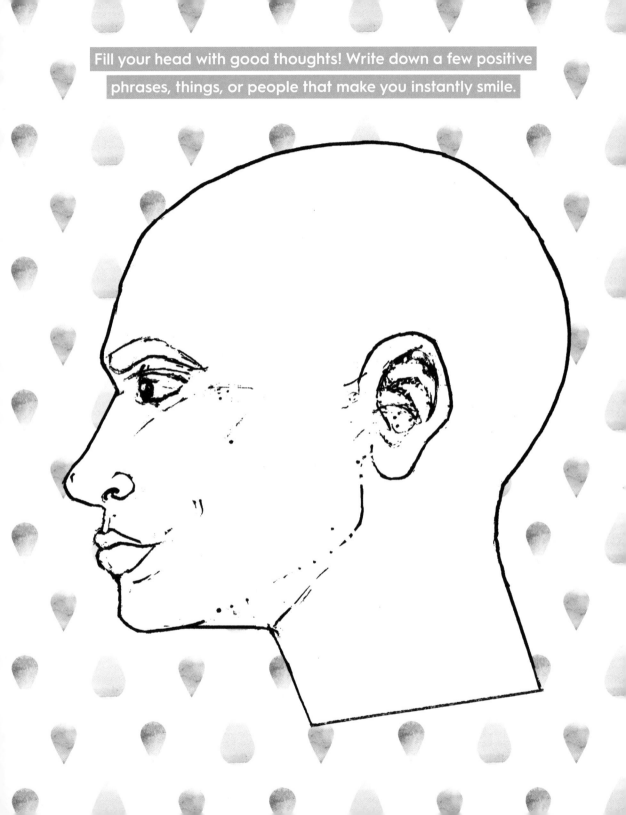

Fill your head with good thoughts! Write down a few positive phrases, things, or people that make you instantly smile.

Sometimes I feel like wearing outfits that are eccentric and unique. Use the stickers at the back of the book to create a zany, totally cool look that you would love to wear.

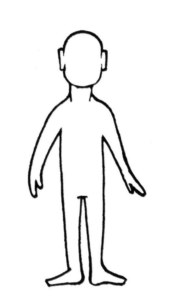

Survive this procrastination maze by navigating through distractions. See if you can catch some Z's.

Sleep is important for your health and creativity.

START

How do you see yourself?

Draw a self-portrait.

Title the drawing.

Write all the important things you love about yourself.

_____

_____

_____

_____

_____

_____

_____

_____

_____

_____

_____

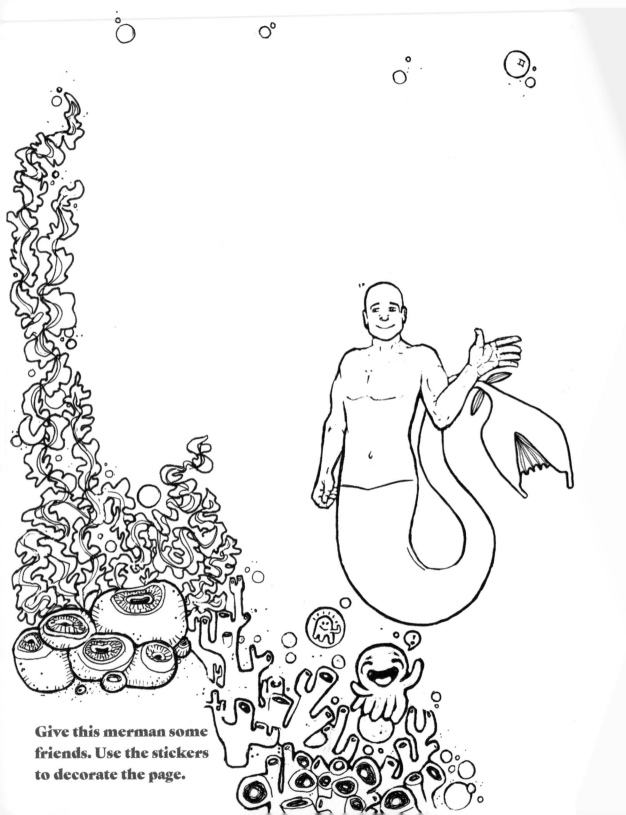

Give this merman some friends. Use the stickers to decorate the page.

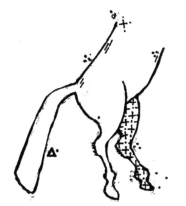

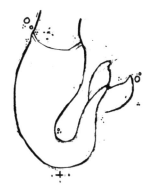

Health is a balance between both the mental and the physical.

What are you doing to take care of yourself? Draw or write those things on each side of the scale.

MENTAL

PHYSICAL

Inspiration is everywhere. Write or draw what inspires you and come back to this page when your creativity runs low. Use the stickers at the back of the book.

**Color in the sneakers and create a
background to show where you would
wear your kicks.**

I love to play the electric guitar. Imagine you could create your own guitar model. What would your guitar be named? How would it look and sound? Finish the poster for your creation.

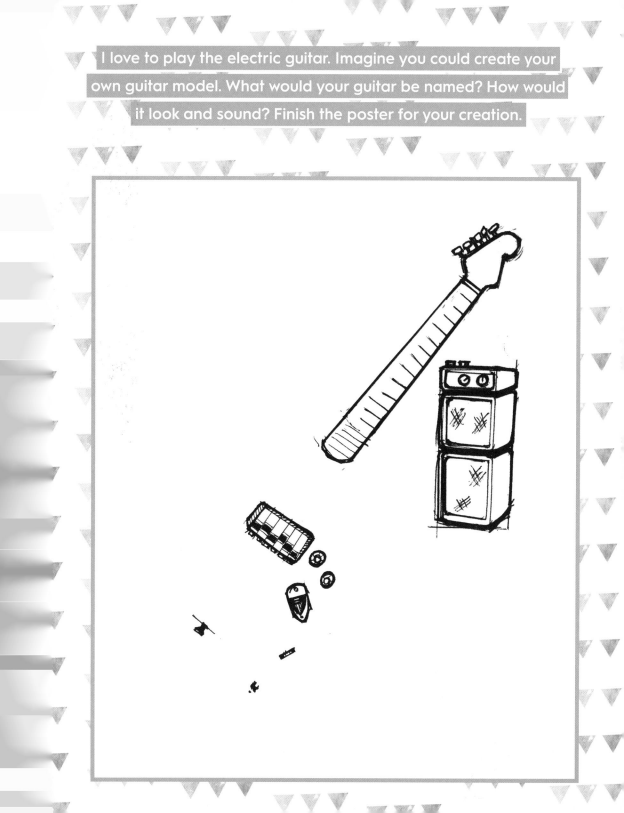

Imagine you made a musical album about your life.

What would your album be called? Design the front cover above.

What would the songs be called?
Write the track list below.

SIDE A

1. _____ 4:52
2. _____ 3:06
3. _____ 2:55
4. _____ 2:33
5. _____ 3:41

SIDE B

1. _____ 5:08
2. _____ 3:15
3. _____ 3:57
4. _____ 2:45
5. _____ 2:55

Create a look that would shake the red carpet.
Use the stickers at the back of the book.

Draw your favorite TV character and your favorite book combined. Title the drawing.

Our expectations are often false. Did you ever imagine a new teacher would look one way . . . and then they looked completely different? Draw your expectation of something below.

EXPECTATION V

Draw its reality below.

REALITY

I spend a lot of time in fictional universes inspired by myths and legends. How many **mythical creatures** do you know? Use these clues to help you solve this puzzle.

DOWN
1. Tinker Bell is the most famous.
2. Half man, half horse.
4. Half woman, half fish.

ACROSS
3. Breathes fire.
5. Has a pot of gold. Wears green.
6. Likes pointy hats . . . and gardens.
7. Like a horse but better.

Answers in the back of the book.

FINISH

hope acceptance positivity transcend

START

Getting past hate and negativity is difficult.
Recognizing it is the first step.
Fight your way through the bad thoughts!

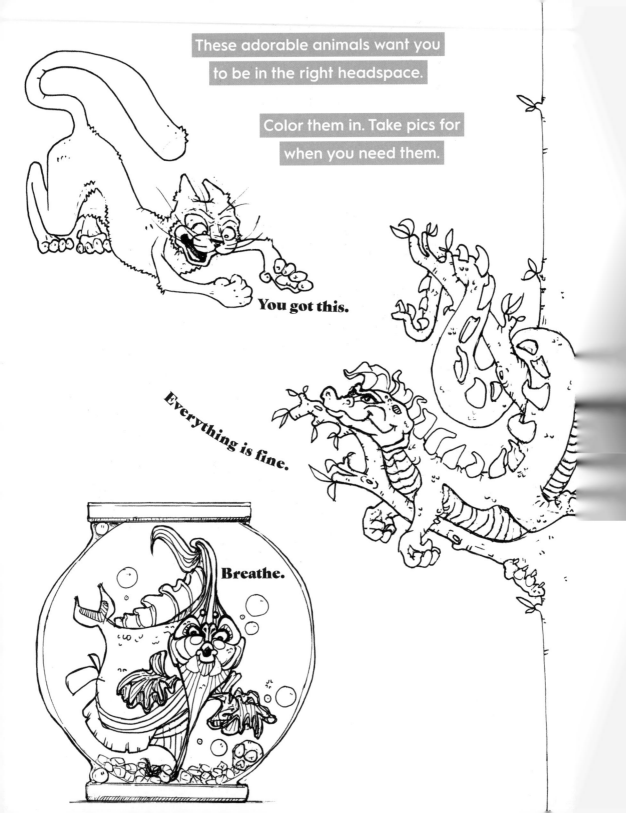

These adorable animals want you to be in the right headspace.

Color them in. Take pics for when you need them.

You got this.

Everything is fine.

Breathe.

Write a word for each letter that represents something important in your life right now. (Ex: For A, it could be ANIMALS.) Come back to these pages in a few years to see what's changed.

A

B

C

D

E

F

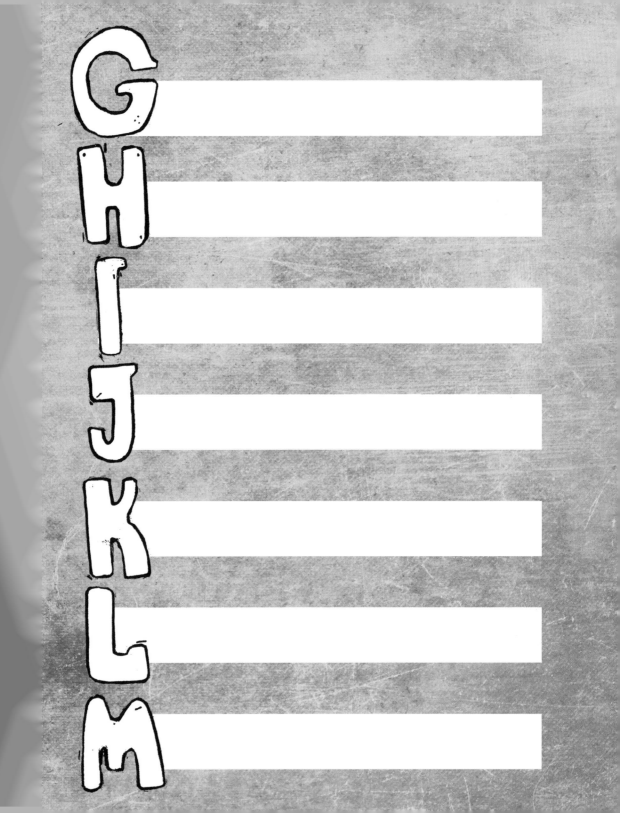

N
O
P
Q
R
S
T

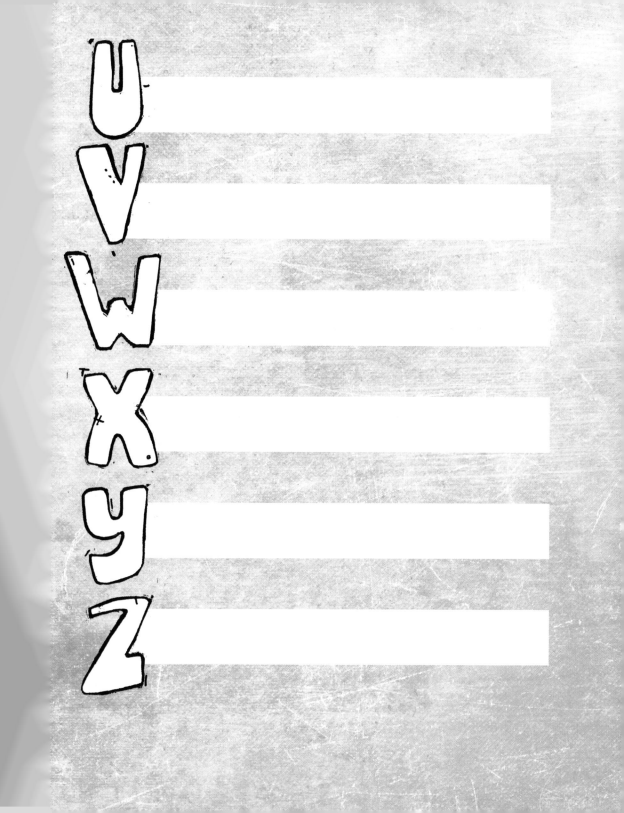

I love personalizing denim with interesting patches.
Use the stickers at the back of the book to decorate this jacket.

The mythological Pegasus is white. Imagine Pegasus got a dye job.
Give him some amazing colors.

What gives you strength? Write or draw the sources.

Use the stickers at the back of the book.

Draw your favorite supervillain and your biggest fear combined.
Title the drawing.

What fills your heart with joy? This treasure map will lead you to the things you love—you just have to fill in the steps along the way.

What are you a fan of?
Pick a book, band, movie, or other fandom and design a T-shirt for your fellow fans.

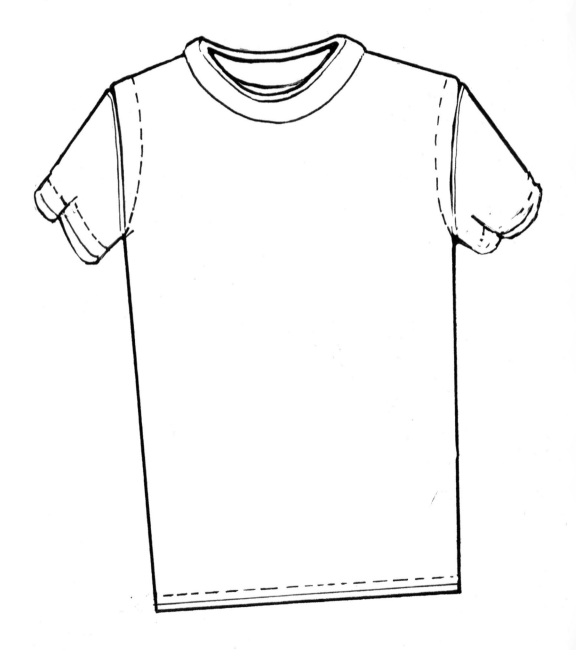

List the reasons you love this fandom.

_____

_____

_____

_____

_____

_____

_____

_____

_____

_____

COLORS   ## TOYS

_____   _____

_____   _____

_____   _____

_____   _____

_____   _____

_____   _____

Now, pick a color from the first list and use it to draw a toy from the second.

Have you seen anything like this before? Why or why not?

Coloring helps me deal with stress.
Create a unique look for each boot. Go crazy.

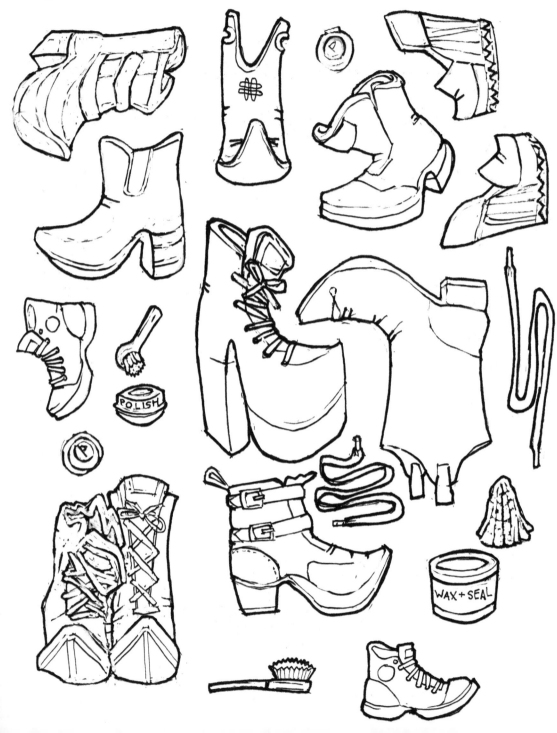

Ukuleles come in all
patterns and colors.
Color each ukulele
differently. Focus on
one ukulele at a time.

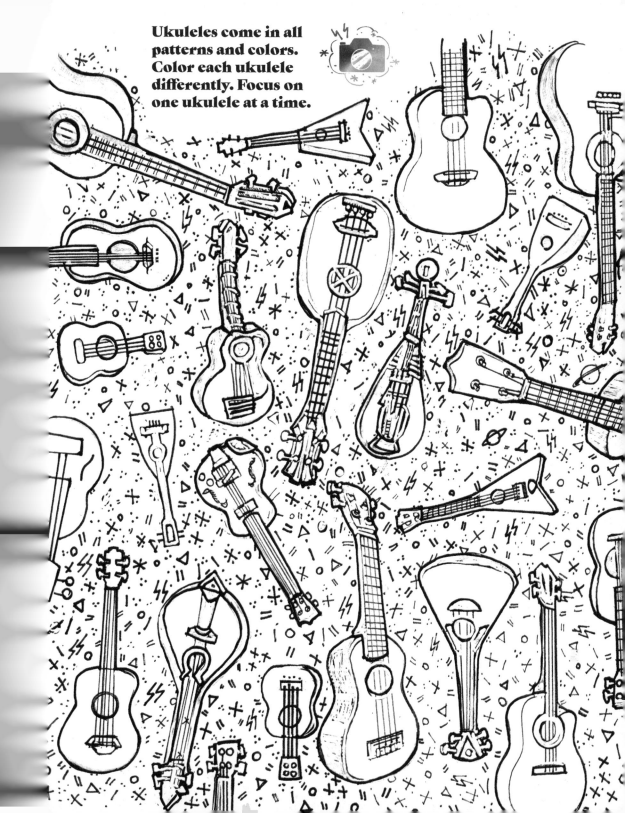

How big of a comic book nerd are you?
Use these clues to help you solve this puzzle.

DOWN
1. Like the Ninja Turtles, X-Men are __ .
3. The D in DC Comics.
5. A style of Japanese comic books and graphic novels.

ACROSS
2. In newspapers you can find a comic __.
4. Kryptonite is his weakness.
6. Spider-Man's real first name.
7. A ___ novel has comic book panels.

Answers in the back of the book.

It takes a lot of work to get to the top.

Design a suit that screams success.

I like to paint my nails in a rainbow pattern.
Give the nails a unique design.

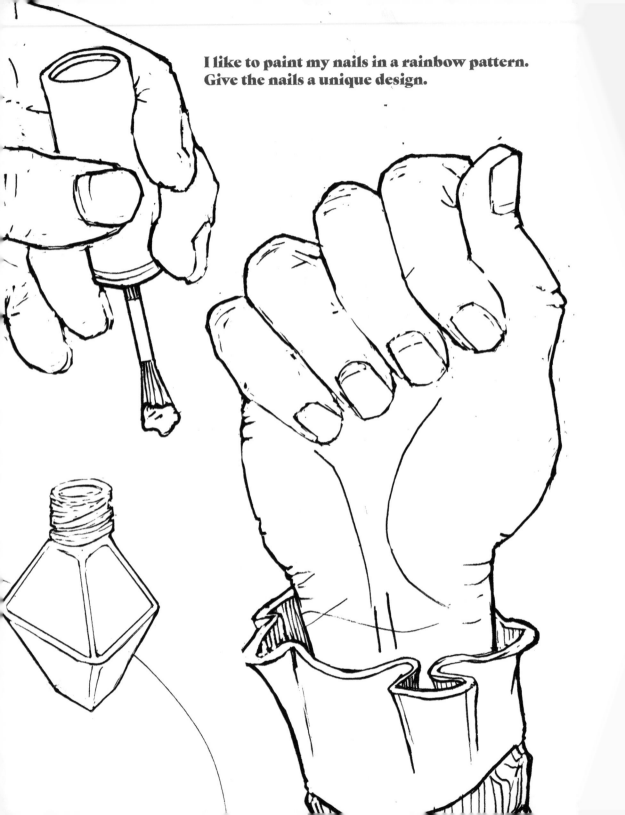

At times of high stress, we can forget that we are loved.

When that happens, it's important to stop and reflect.

What makes you feel loved? Write or draw your thoughts below.

Use the stickers at the back of the book.

MY FAMILY TREE

Our families influence us in so many ways. Here are a few members of my family.

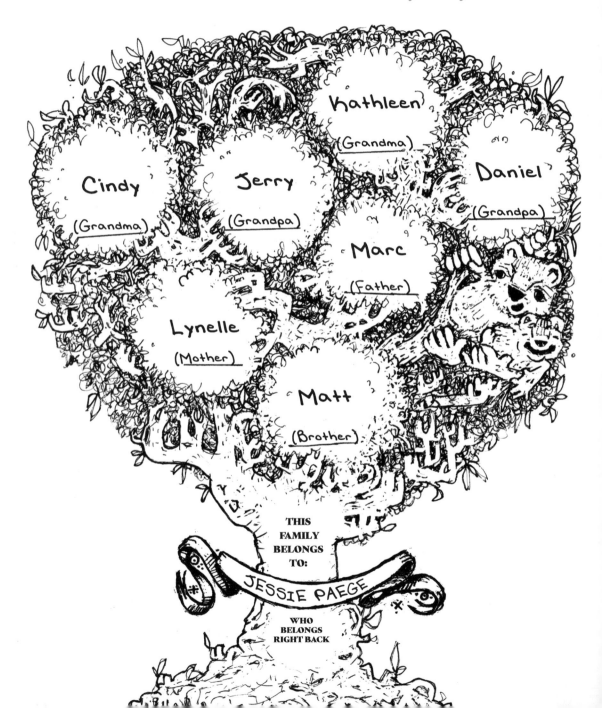

Kathleen (Grandma)

Cindy (Grandma)

Jerry (Grandpa)

Daniel (Grandpa)

Marc (Father)

Lynelle (Mother)

Matt (Brother)

THIS FAMILY BELONGS TO:

JESSIE PAEGE

WHO BELONGS RIGHT BACK

Here are a few of the many lessons my family has taught me.

Brother: Don't be ashamed of your interests, even if no one else shares them.

Dad: Nothing can cheat hard work.

Mother: Kindness is the most attractive quality in a person.

Grandma: Don't bottle up emotions. Express how you feel.

Grandpa: Strength is one of the most attractive things.

YOUR FAMILY TREE

Fill in your own family tree with people who are important to you. Keep in mind that families can be made up of more than just blood. Every family is different!

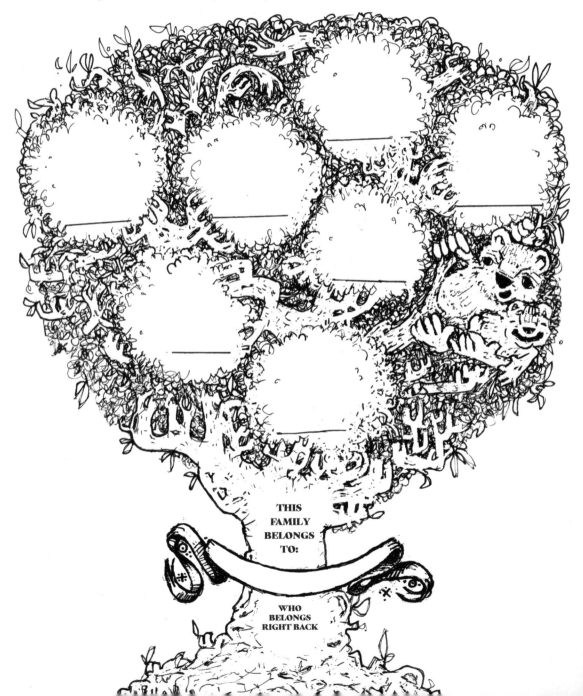

THIS
FAMILY
BELONGS
TO:

WHO
BELONGS
RIGHT BACK

**List a few things you've learned
from the people on your family tree.**

_____

_____

_____

_____

_____

_____

_____

_____

_____

_____

Make your favorite book your own.

Design a new cover for a story you love.

Show the parts you like the best.

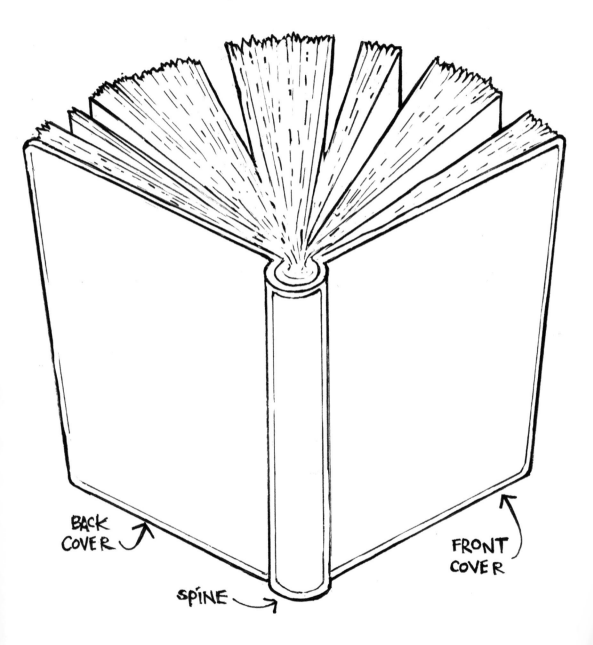

BACK COVER

FRONT COVER

SPINE

Now make the book even better!
Write what you would want to add
to or change about the story.

_____

_____

_____

_____

_____

_____

_____

_____

_____

_____

_____

_____

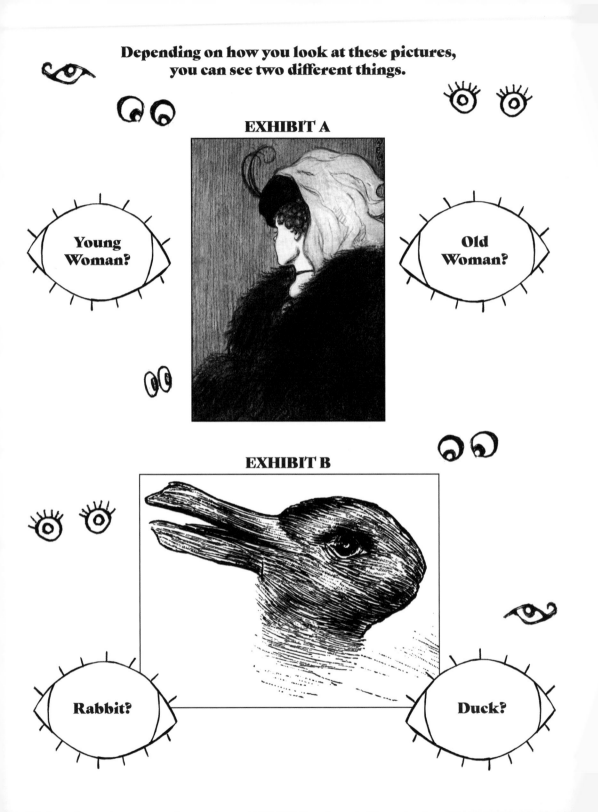

Depending on how you look at these pictures, you can see two different things.

EXHIBIT A

Young Woman?

Old Woman?

EXHIBIT B

Rabbit?

Duck?

Now draw your own optical illusion.
#prochallenge

This book needs narwhals.
Color them in to create an amazing pattern.

What makes you feel fear? Write or draw your thoughts below. Recognizing fears is important and will help with getting rid of them. Use the stickers at the back of the book.

I started getting pink highlights in my hair for breast cancer awareness.

Then I decided to try dyeing all of my hair pink, and I fell in love with it.

Now I change my hair color whenever I feel like it.

I define my appearance. My appearance doesn't define me.

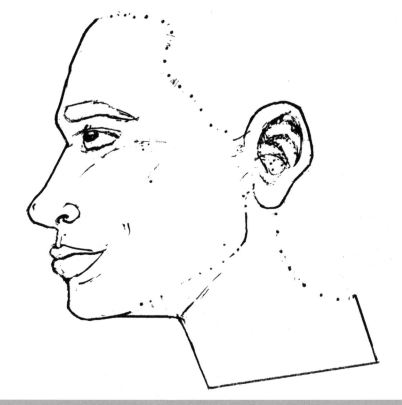

If you could dye your hair any color, what color would you choose?
Draw your dream style above and color it in.

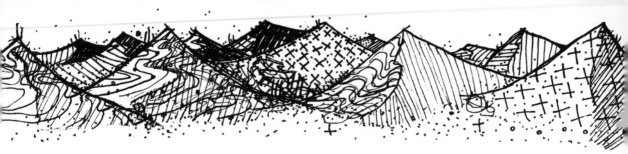

Draw an oasis where everything you love grows on trees. Come back here whenever you need to chill out.

Draw your favorite superhero and favorite teacher combined.

Title your drawing.

Anime is awesome! Use these clues to help you solve this puzzle.

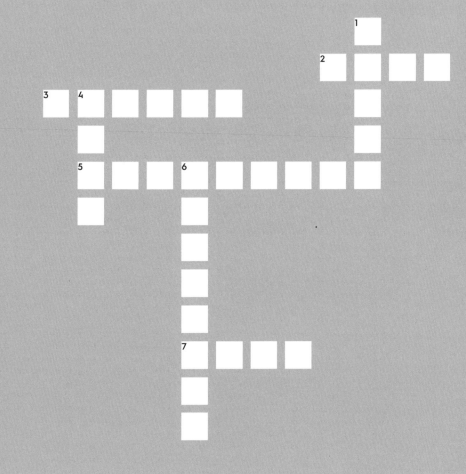

DOWN
1. Anime is from this country.
4. Hayao Miyazaki directed *Spirited* __.
6. The name Pokémon comes from "pocket __".

ACROSS
2. *Dragon* __ *Z* stars Guko and Gohan.
3. __ Moon protects earth as a Sailor Soldier.
5. Anime is short for this word.
7. Good vs. __

Answers in the back of the book.

I love when people express their individuality.

Color in the unique styles.
Give the people unique names.

Say something wherever you go.
Use the stickers at the back of the book
to personalize this board.

They say unicorns are unique.
Color each of these differently.

I can't live without music, whether it's playing the electric guitar or listening to records. How do you incorporate music into your life? Write or draw your thoughts below. Use the stickers at the back of the book.

Draw your favorite food and favorite car combined.

Title your drawing.

You've heard this question a million times:
What do you want to be when you grow up?

Well, what if you want to be more than one thing?
Fill in these business cards with your
dream occupations. Taglines welcome!
Use the stickers at the back of the book.

Don't you wish your life was as simple as a fairy tale sometimes?

Use these clues to help you solve this puzzle.

DOWN

1. He's *hopping* to be kissed.
2. She's often saved whether she needs it or not.
3. It can be cast by a witch.
5. Where the royal family lives.

ACROSS

4. The Disney princess with the longest hair.
6. Cinderella left this behind.
7. Must learn to love to break the spell.

Answers in the back of the book.

Help this mer-kid get to her mer-family.

These creatures need scales.
Draw interesting patterns
and color them in.

What makes you feel your best? Write or draw your thoughts below.

Use the stickers at the back of the book.

Design a uniform for the school of your dreams.

Write the top 10 rules for
your dream school.

1. _____

2. _____

3. _____

4. _____

5. _____

6. _____

7. _____

8. _____

9. _____

10. _____

I am your father. Use these clues to help you solve this sci-fi puzzle.

DOWN
1. R2-D2 is this type of robot.
3. Madeleine L'Engle wrote *A Wrinkle in* __.
4. E.T. just wants to __ home.
6. Transformers are alien __.

ACROSS
2. You'll find Captain Kirk on the __ Enterprise.
5. A car is a time machine in *Back to the* __.
7. The color of Doctor Who's time machine.

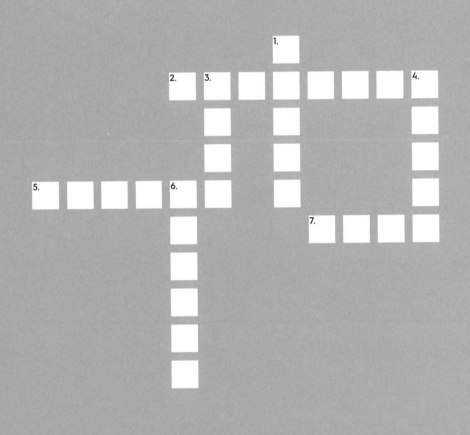

Answers in the back of the book.

Imagine your life is a video game. What would it look like?

Draw the main characters, their tools, their power-ups, and extra lives.

TOOLS:

POWER-UPS:

CHARACTER SELECT:

LIVES:

Create your own campaign poster
with a tagline that you **believe** in.

Use the stickers at the back of the book.

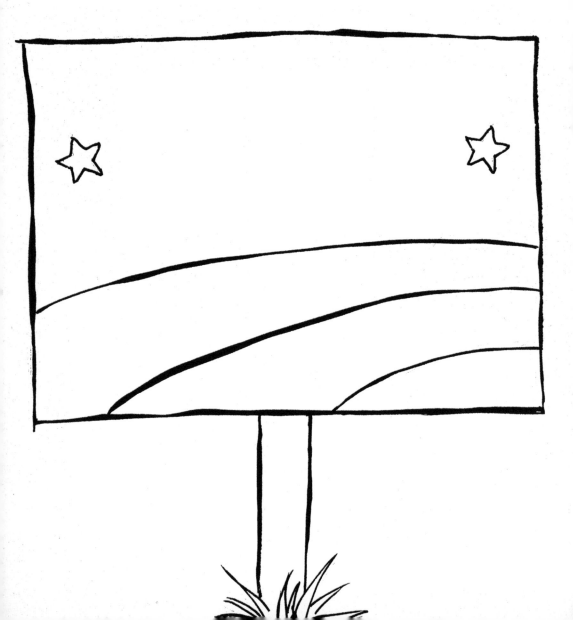

**Write down the top three things
you'd do once you're in charge.**

1. _____

_____

2. _____

_____

3. _____

_____

What will the phone of the future look like? Draw your phone today and what you imagine your phone will be like in 50 years.

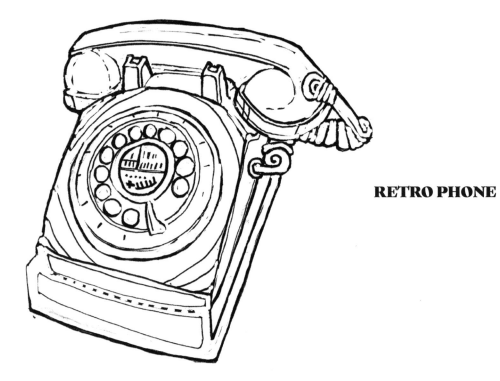

RETRO PHONE

YOUR PHONE NOW

FUTURE PHONE

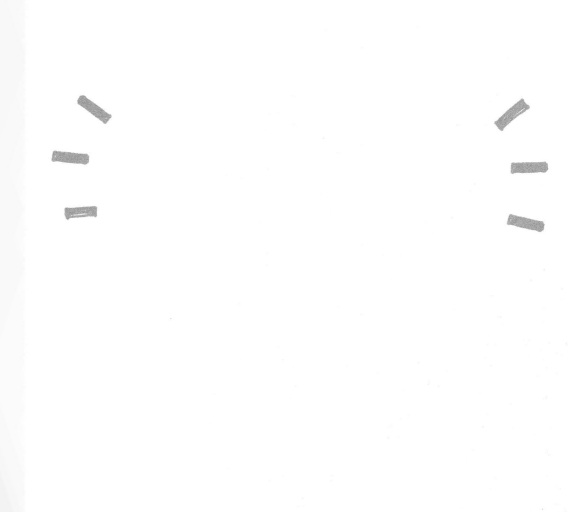

I like dragons.
This one is a peaceful creature.
Color in this dainty dude.

This time machine needs some color!

If you could go back in time and tell your younger self three things, what you would say? Write those three things in the space below.

1.

2.

3.

This is your fairy tale.
What do the floating
lanterns represent?

Wishes, worries, a cry for help?
Color in the scene.

What are you most thankful for? Write or draw your thoughts below.

Use the stickers at the back of the book.

ANSWER PAEGE

MYTHICAL CREATURES CROSSWORD

DOWN
1. FAIRY
2. CENTAUR
4. MERMAID

ACROSS
3. DRAGON
5. LEPRECHAUN
6. GNOME
7. UNICORN

COMIC BOOK CROSSWORD

DOWN
1. MUTANTS
3. DETECTIVE
5. MANGA

ACROSS
2. STRIP
4. SUPERMAN
6. PETER
7. GRAPHIC

ANIME CROSSWORD

DOWN
1. JAPAN
4. AWAY
6. MONSTERS

ACROSS
2. BALL
3. SAILOR
5. ANIMATION
7. EVIL

FAIRY TALE CROSSWORD

DOWN
1. THE FROG PRINCE
2. PRINCESS
3. SPELL
5. CASTLE

ACROSS
4. RAPUNZEL
6. GLASS SLIPPER
7. BEAST

SCI-FI CROSSWORD

DOWN
1. DROID
3. TIME
4. PHONE
6. ROBOTS

ACROSS
2. STARSHIP
5. FUTURE
7. BLUE

ABOUT THE AUTHOR PAEGE

- I am the host of a lifestyle, comedy, and advice channel on YouTube, @JessiePaege.

- I grew up in New Jersey. My family resides in Florida, and I'm now in California.

- I barely spoke until third grade. I was only able to talk to three people: my parents and my brother. My confidence has since grown like crazy, and I've become a new person. It's still me, but I'm able to communicate more confidently now.

- English and math were my absolute favorite subjects in school.

- I was made fun of in third grade for pretending to be a mermaid and a spy during lunchtime. As an 18-year-old, I embrace that side of myself even more.

- I love memes. Enough said.

- I started my YouTube channel when I was 15 years old. My username was @glamwithjessie. If you couldn't tell . . . a lot has changed since then.

- Some things you'll find in my apartment: a giant rainbow painted on a wall, a giant rainbow Slinky, a lava lamp, a gumball machine, a dinosaur cookie jar, and a watermelon candle. Just the necessities.

- I learned to play guitar when I was 10 years old. I play both electric and acoustic, but I really love the electric guitar.

FIND ME HERE

YOUTUBE

youtube.com/jessiepaege

youtube.com/paegetwo

INSTRAGRAM

@jessiepaege

@jessietrash

TWITTER

@jessiepaege

LOOK FOR MY FIRST BOOK!

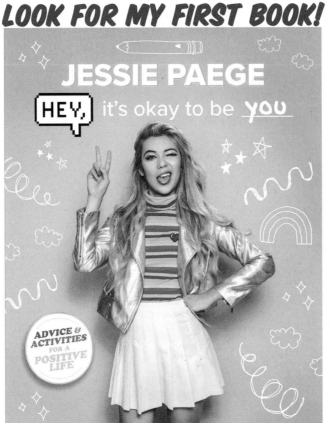